Obedience

Kenneth Hagin Jr.

Eighth Printing 1998

ISBN 0-89276-720-0

In the U.S. write:
Kenneth Hagin Ministries
P.O. Box 50126
Tulsa, OK 74150-0126

In Canada write:
Kenneth Hagin Ministries
P.O. Box 335, Station D
Etobicoke (Toronto), Ontario
Canada, M9A 4X3

The Life of
Obedience

Contents

Chapter 1
Why Should I Obey?

There is a subject in today's world that is not very popular. It is also not a popular subject in Charismatic ranks. In fact, it is not a popular subject in *any* rank. And it is spelled "O-B-E-D-I-E-N-C-E." Obedience.

It seems as though you can talk about anything you want as long as it doesn't involve adhering to a set of laws, rules, or regulations. Maybe one reason that people don't like to talk about obedience is because, in the past, "obedience" did carry a negative connotation; it was always, "Don't do this," and "Don't do that." And in that context, obedience was used more often than not to indicate an adherence to a set of rules and regulations which were not *necessarily* in line with the Word of God. These were really the do's and the don'ts of tradition. But when you actually begin to study the subject, *obedience is the underlying theme of the entire Word of God*. How pertinent this subject is to the Church today!

You cannot even receive salvation without obedience. That's true! You have to obey God and come in line with His Word in order to accept Christ as your Savior.

In Genesis we see obedience and disobedience through God's perspective as Adam's sons came to worship God. Abel conformed to God's laws and brought the proper animal sacrifice as he was supposed to according to God's instructions. But Cain wanted to come to God in his own way. He wanted to be recognized and approved by God bringing the sacrifice *his way* — not God's way — and yet *still receive* the blessings of God!

So Cain, being a farmer, brought the work of his own hands — the fruits of the ground — and offered them on the altar. But God refused his sacrifice. Why? Because God told man from the beginning how to please Him, and therefore, receive from Him. So Cain's own disobedience made receiving from God absolutely impossible.

You will notice in the Old Testament, no one ever got in trouble unless they disobeyed the Word of God. The same is true in the New Testament. And today, we don't get in trouble unless we disobey the Word of God. Of course you realize that God's Word is His law. Therefore, simply stated, the underlying theme of the Word of God is obedience with no negotiations.

Many people have trouble with this. They say, for example, that they cannot keep the Ten Commandments. But really you don't have to worry about the Ten Commandments if you'll just remember one commandment: "Obey what God says!"

God is the Creator of all things. He is the only One who can set into motion the laws of His Word, and we have no right or authority to negotiate with Him when it comes to those laws. God is the Final Authority.

Usually people who are having difficulty lining up with God's Word are those who didn't really want to obey God in the first place. They wanted to find a compromise — a loophole — in the Word of God. But God is not a God of compromise with respect to His own Word. With God it's "yea" or "nay"; with some Christians it's "maybe-so."

But you see, God has been specific in His Word so that we would have a clear-cut path or highway to follow; one in which there would be no confusion. The road signs in God's Word are not confusing, but straightforward. Furthermore, they will always lead us to victory, and eventually to Heaven. Simply put, those road signs state, "Obey God in His Word!"

Obedience — lining up with God in His Word — is not a popular subject in this day and age, but it is a vital one to the Body of Christ; therefore; it is something we need to look at more carefully.

As a scriptural setting, let's turn to First Samuel 15:1, *"Samuel also said unto Saul, The Lord sent me to anoint thee to be king over his people, over Israel: now therefore HEARKEN thou unto the voice of the words of the Lord."*

Samuel is telling Saul to *listen carefully* to what God is saying and then be sure to *do it*! That's what "hearken" means.

Then Samuel went on to tell Saul what the Lord of hosts said to do: *"Thus saith the Lord of hosts, I remember that which Amalek did to Israel, how he laid wait for him in the way, when he came up from Egypt. Now go and smite Amalek, and utterly destroy ALL that they have, and spare them not; but slay both man and woman, infant and suckling, ox and sheep, camel and ass"* (1 Sam. 15:2,3).

But instead of obeying the Lord, we read in verse 9: *"But Saul and the people spared Agag, and the best of the sheep, and of the oxen, and of the fatlings, and the lambs, and all that was good, and would not utterly destroy them: but every thing that was vile and refuse, that they destroyed utterly."*

To get the full impact of this story, and to understand the real nature of Saul's disobedience, you must realize exactly how Saul sinned. After Saul had gone out to battle, he had done what the law normally required of him. When Israel won a battle, they were required to bring back sacrifices to offer to God for the victory. We might call this "a thanksgiving offering."

At any other time, King Saul would have been acting correctly according to the law's demands. Also, in battles of that day, the victor was entitled to the spoils of war: All the cattle, horses, chariots, and gold. Everything that could be salvaged could be rightfully taken by the conquering army.

Furthermore, it was customary for the conquering king to

take the enemy king alive and parade him in triumph through the streets of the major cities. This was considered one of the greatest tokens of prestige for a conquering king; it gave him great credibility, not just among his own people, but in the sight of other nations as well.

There was only one problem in Saul's case, God had commanded him: *Bring nothing back!* Saul was not to bring back the enemy king, nor animals for sacrifice, nor any spoils of war!

Now, of course, no disobedience is hidden from the Lord. So Saul's disobedience did not go unobserved by Him: *"Then came the word of the Lord unto Samuel, saying, It repenteth me that I have set up Saul to be king: for he is turned back from following me, and hath not performed my commandments. And it grieved*

Samuel; and he cried unto the Lord all night" (1 Sam. 15:10,11).

Why did the Lord regret making Saul the king of Israel? *Disobedience!* He failed to obey the voice of the Lord!

To bring this into perspective, how do you suppose God feels now, when His very own children disobey Him? That's a sobering thought!

First, Saul openly disobeyed the commands of the Lord. Then, when confronted by Samuel, Saul compounded his sin by lying, for he said, ". . . *Blessed be thou* [Samuel] *of the Lord: I have performed the commandment of the Lord*" (v. 13). But Samuel, the wise, old servant of the Lord, responded, ". . . *What meaneth then this bleating of the sheep in mine ears, and the lowing of the oxen which I hear?*" (v. 14).

Notice the next incident, Saul began to blame the people. "*And*

*Saul said, THEY have brought
them from the Amalekites: for
THE PEOPLE spared the best of
the sheep and of the oxen, to sacrifice unto the Lord thy God; and
the rest we have utterly destroyed"*
(v. 15).

Now this is a very strange
thing for the king of Israel to say,
because in fact, *the people were
subject to him.* But Saul needed
someone else to take the blame,
so he conveniently tried to cover
his initial disobedience to God by
blaming the people.

Saul then lied the second time,
strongly affirming to Samuel that
he had obeyed the Lord:

1 SAMUEL 15:17-23
**17 And Samuel said, When
thou wast little in thine
own sight, wast thou not
made the head of the tribes
of Israel, and the Lord
anointed thee king over
Israel?**

18 And the Lord sent thee on a journey, and said, Go and utterly destroy the sinners the Amalekites, and fight against them until they be consumed.

19 Wherefore then didst thou not obey the voice of the Lord, but didst fly upon the spoil, and didst evil in the sight of the Lord?

20 And Saul said unto Samuel, Yea, I have obeyed the voice of the Lord [this is the second time Saul lied], and have gone the way which the Lord sent me, and have brought Agag the king of Amalek, and have utterly destroyed the Amalekites.

21 BUT THE PEOPLE took of the spoil, sheep and oxen, the chief of the things which should have been utterly destroyed, to sacrifice unto the Lord thy God in Gilgal.

22 And Samuel said, Hath the Lord as great delight in burnt offerings and sacrifices, as in obeying the voice

of the Lord? Behold, to
OBEY is better than sacrifice, and to HEARKEN than
the fat of rams.
23 For rebellion is as the sin
of witchcraft, and stubborn-
ness is as iniquity and idol-
atry. Because thou hast
rejected the WORD OF THE
LORD, he hath also rejected
thee from being king.

Samuel actually was saying,
"It would be better for you to obey
the voice of the Lord than to sacrifice to God — even in the most
precise and correct manner —
because your sacrificing done
without obedience to all that God
has said, will really ascend up to
His nostrils as a stench!"

God delights in sacrifices, all
right, but He does not delight in
them when you haven't obeyed.
What God really delights in,
above all else, is obedience to His
Word.

Therefore, God *had* to refuse Saul's sacrifice just as He had to refuse Cain's offering. Both were sacrifices done in disobedience to all that God had said.

How does this pertain to us today?

There are a lot of people in the Church world today who are involved in a similar type of disobedience, and may not realize it.

For example, they may be making faith confessions, and trying to say all the "right things," when actually God cannot *bless* them because they failed to obey His voice in other areas. What God is really wanting from them is their complete obedience.

Let's bring this even closer to home. There are a lot of Christians putting their faith out to believe God for finances, for example. But, on the other hand, they are actually robbing God, and are therefore in no position to receive God's blessing at all! How are they robbing God? By not paying their tithes! And remember the principle, "To obey is better than sacrifice," or "confess," or "fast," or *whatever*.

If someone is in disobedience to God's Word — I don't care how much they confess the Word, or how much they pray, or how much they fast — the full promise of God cannot come to them. They may receive a little return from all their confessing and believing. But until they start to obey God's Word, *the full blessing of God* cannot be theirs.

You can pray and sing all you want to, but if God has told you to do something, and you're refusing to do it, there is no way God can bless and honor you. *Your own disobedience has made receiving from God absolutely impossible*!

Obedience to God's Word is what will give you peace on the

inside in the midst of the storm. When you obey God to the fullest, He will take care of you. Whether it's in the spiritual realm or the natural realm, obedience to God is the thing that will see you through. Obedience will *always* bring you victory. Obedience to God will allow you to lay down and sleep at night without any worry. When I've fully obeyed God, why should I fret? Why should I worry? Why should I lose sleep? Because when I know I've obeyed — then I know God's got it all under control!

That may be why some people are still wringing their hands *after* they've prayed, have trouble sleeping at night, and are always crying, "What are we going to do now?" It may be that they know there is an area where they have not completely yielded to God and obeyed Him. And because they have not completely obeyed, God's promises cannot fully be theirs. So they have a reason to worry. They have a reason to be upset. *The only condition to remaining in the blessings of God, is to remain in obedience to God!*

You see, there are people who are in the so-called "faith walk" who are making faith confessions which are never going to be answered. They are talking the "right" talk. They are quoting the "right" scriptures. And the people around them are probably wondering why God is not meeting their faith. Yet in their hearts these same Christians may know exactly why they are not receiving from God.

It may be that God has told them to do something which they have utterly refused to do. And yet to all outward appearances they are walking in the "perfect will of God." But realize that a person cannot be walking in the perfect will of God if he's not walking in obedience!

There are a lot of Christians today who are going to church every time the door is open, reading their Bibles and praying, and yet it all seems to little avail — *because they themselves are short-circuiting the power of God in their lives.* The disobedience somewhere in their lives nullifies the rest of their efforts. Disobedience cannot bring blessings from God; but disobedience will eventually bring judgment from God.

God is saying specific things to each member of the Body of Christ. And yet many are telling the Lord *what* they are going to do for Him, and *how* they are going to do it. That's why we need to understand what obedience really is. It is crucial to the Body of Christ for the day and the hour in which we live.

Chapter 2
Obedience: More Than an Action

The first thing we need to realize about obedience is that it is a life principle. That means obedience isn't just a single act, or even a series of *actions*. Obedience is a whole lifestyle characterized by a spirit of obedience, or a *habitual attitude* of obedience.

Jesus, our Example, demonstrated this attitude and lifestyle of obedience. His whole reason for coming to earth was, ". . . *Lo, I come to do thy will, O God . . .*" (Heb. 10:9). The principle by which He lived His entire life was obedience. And we, as His Body — fulfilling His will upon the earth — will have to live by this same principle.

In fact, if we're ever going to accomplish anything in this life for God as Spirit-filled, faith-believing, faith-confessing, Bible-toting, Word-quoting children of God, the number one principle we must live by, is obedience.

Yet it seems that when the word "obedience" is mentioned, some Christians get a long face. Actually, obedience should be the Christian's greatest joy because God said, *"If ye be WILLING and OBEDIENT, ye shall eat the good of the land"* (Isa. 1:19). It's interesting to note that everyone is willing to eat the good of the land, but not everyone is willing to be obedient. What a vast difference between the two!

Another thing we need to recognize, is that in true obedience there is an element of real humility. An obedient person is also a humble person. Why? Because he puts the will and the desires of the one he serves above his own will and his own desires.

Now there are many Christians who will try to prove to you how *humble* they are. And though they may not say it in words, the attitude they portray is, *"I'll show you* just how humble I am." But that's not humility.

You see, we need to have the same mind which was in Christ Jesus. Jesus emptied Himself, and took on the form of a servant, humbling Himself to the point of death on a cross. That's how complete His humility and obedience was.

And the scriptures say, *"Let this mind be in you, which was also in Christ Jesus: Who, being in the form of God, thought it not robbery TO BE EQUAL WITH God: But made HIMSELF OF NO REPUTATION, and took upon him the FORM OF A SERVANT, and was made in the likeness of men*" (Phil. 2:5-7).

Jesus Christ, the Son of God, became a Servant. He took the servant's role. Yet in Christendom today, there are too many people who do not want the lowly position of the servant. They want an exalted position of recognition and importance.

And if they're in the ministry, they want a big tape ministry and a huge book ministry, so they can receive acclaim. But to have the mind of Christ is to have the humility and obedience of a servant.

Think about that word "servant." If you're a servant, you know your role. A servant doesn't ask questions, or argue about the commands given to him. He knows he's there only to serve the one in charge.

Being a servant is of vital importance to the Body of Christ.

But because of the way some people were raised, it is hard for them to understand and adapt to the attitude of a servant. They are afraid that if they do, it will put them right back into the lowly state from which they came before they were saved. But remember, that was in the devil's kingdom — under his evil tyranny. That's not how it is in the Kingdom of God under the rule of the King of kings.

God's Kingdom is ruled by faith and love. The rule of that tyrant and enemy — Satan — is a rule of hate, distrust, and unbelief. In Satan's kingdom, the individual is nothing.

But under God's rule, when we become servants, we actually become someone! When we become subject to God the Father and bow before Him through the Lord Jesus Christ, then God Himself lifts us up and seats us with

Christ. "*And hath raised us up together, and made us sit together in heavenly places in Christ Jesus*" (Eph. 2:6).

Notice that in God's Kingdom, humble obedience allows us to rule with Jesus Christ! And with God it's that attitude of humility which is so important. Our *attitude* is *all* important. So many Christians miss the *attitude*.

To give an example, the reason why some Christians are not receiving a return from their giving is because the attitude with which they are giving is not right before God. It's not that they are failing to give; it's that they're giving with the *wrong* attitude. Their attitude seems to be, "God, I'm doing this for You, so You owe me!" But God doesn't owe you anything! *You* owe God everything! Because you are nothing without Him!

So we see that obedience is more than what some have

thought. It is not *just* an act, even a series of actions, or just something that we do or don't do. Obedience is more than that. It is a complete lifestyle; a life principle or attitude of heart by which to live.

How, then, does obedience relate to faith?

People like to talk about faith, yet many times they do not realize that to have strong faith, they must be obedient to the Word of God. The two — faith and obedience — are inseparable. It's not just a one-time confession of faith that gets the job done; it's a lifestyle of obedience to, and faith in, the Word of God that gets the job done.

So often we hear it said in Christian circles that faith is just a matter of "believing God." "Just believe," they say. However, a study of the Word of God will actually show that every promise in the Word of God carries with it a commitment for *us* to do something. In other words, every time we *believe* God and make a confession of faith, we are putting ourselves in a position to exercise obedience. *It's never a matter of God or His Word failing; it's a matter of whether or not we are in line for His blessings!*

An example of this relationship between faith and obedience is found in Mark chapter 11.

MARK 11:23,24
23 For verily I say unto you, That whosoever shall say unto this mountain, Be thou removed, and be thou cast into the sea; and shall not doubt in his heart, but shall believe that those things which he saith shall come to pass; he shall have whatsoever he saith.
24 Therefore I say unto you, What things soever ye desire, when ye pray, believe that ye

**receive them, and ye shall
have them.**

Now usually when we read
this familiar passage, we stop at
verse 24. But before verse 23 and
24 will even work, we will have to
OBEY verse 25. We don't read
this verse as frequently, because
it's not the part that thrills us,
but it says: *"And when ye stand
praying, FORGIVE, if ye have
ought against any . . . ."* That
means if you are holding a grudge
whatsoever against anyone — forgive him, *". . . that your Father
also which is in heaven may forgive you your trespasses."*

There are Christians who
quote Mark 11:23 and 24, and yet
nothing happens. Then they wonder why their faith isn't working,
or question why the Word isn't
working for them. But it's because
they still remember a time when
someone wronged them. And they

have never forgiven that person,
nor forgotten it!

*We must realize that we cannot
move into this area of great faith
without walking in the love of God
and in complete obedience to His
Word.* It's impossible.

Galatians 5:6 says that faith
works by love, and, therefore, our
faith will not work. In fact, the
more I study obedience, the more
I am convinced that faith and
love cannot operate without it!
When you love God, the things of
God, the Body of Christ, and
you're in complete obedience to
God's Word — *there's absolutely
nothing that can stand in your
way and hinder your faith!*

When you, as a member of the
Body of Christ, are in line with
God's Word and obeying Him on a
daily, consistent basis, *then* the
good things of God will be able to
come to you in abundance. *Then*
First Peter 2:24 will become

effective in your life on a continual basis. *Then* Philippians 4:19 will become a daily reality to you. *Then* Luke 6:38 will become a permanent part of your life. *All the promises of God's Word will become yours, as you obey the counsel of God in His Word.*

Some Christians have wondered why the power of God is not manifested in their lives. But without obedience, God cannot trust us with His power! It is when we come in line with His Word in every area of our lives, that God can trust us. Then we are no longer out to serve ourselves, but we are dedicated to His service.

The whole of God's plan is based on serving God in obedience to *His will*, not our own. We talk a lot about serving God, but are we really servants? A servant will do whatever his master tells him to do: It makes no difference what it is.

A minister related this story to me once, which shows the attitude some in the Body of Christ may have toward serving.

A preacher had just finished his sermon, and had taken his coat off, since it was very hot. He handed his coat to someone standing nearby to hold for him, until he was ready to put it back on. The man he handed the coat to rudely retorted, "I'm not your servant! I don't have to hold your coat!"

Now if that had been Jesus, Jesus would not only have held the preacher's coat, but He would have patted him on the back too! You see, Jesus was the servant of *all*.

In fact, Jesus had such a servant's heart that He performed one of the lowliest tasks of that day: He washed His disciples' feet. That was probably one of the most humbling jobs a servant could have — to wash the feet of those who had been walking the dusty roads.

When we see Jesus' attitude of serving others, we begin to realize that until we are *willing* and *obedient* to be a good servant as Jesus was, there is no way we can eat the good of the land.

Yes, we can sing about who we are in Christ Jesus. We can sing about being kings and priests unto God. We can sing about being adopted into the family of God — and what an exalted position it is to be seated in heavenly places with Christ Jesus. We can pray and make our confessions about who we are in Christ and what we have as Kingdom rights. But until we are willing to be a servant just like our Elder Brother, and bend our knee to serve God and the Body of Christ — there is no way we are really in complete obedience to God. I'm talking about a spiritual attitude as well as actions!

Let me say it another way: If we become obedient unto the servant's position, we *will* eat the good of the land.

Yes, in Christ we are someone. Yes, in Christ we do reign and rule as kings and priests. *But we also need to realize that we are still the SERVANTS of the Most High.* We will never get too important to be a servant; Jesus never did.

We must realize the high place being a servant holds in God's sight. His Son was a Servant. If those Christians who have felt that being a servant was too lowly a position for them, would pray: "Lord, I want to do Your will; just show me what to do and I will obey," God would give them such joy in obedience. And they would find that obstacles would melt away in their lives, and circumstances which seemed as if they would never change, would begin to move out of the way.

Remember, the Bible doesn't just say when you're *obedient* you will eat the good of the land; it says you will eat the good of the land when you are WILLING AND OBEDIENT! Get willing! Confess, "Lord, I will obey You! Lord, I will be Your servant. Lord, I will serve You. Lord, I will let the same mind be in me which was in Christ Jesus."

Chapter 3
Obtaining Your Promised Land

The Body of Christ must realize that if we are ever going to fulfill every promise of God in our own lives, and be able to come into our "promised land," then we will have to learn how to completely obey God.

The "land of promise" for the Christian is what God has promised to us in His Word. The Bible tells us about every good thing that already belongs to us. And these promises are our "Canaan" — or promised land. We enter into the richness of our promised land in just the same way the children of Israel were supposed to enter into theirs — through obedience.

Some think it's burdensome and difficult to live a good Christian life, and that obedience is a hard taskmaster. Actually, the opposite is true! Disobedience is the hard taskmaster, and all of our difficulties arise from *not* obeying God. Disobedience allows the devil to bring things against our lives, and it's not God's fault at all. A lot of people would like to blame God for some of their troubles, when actually it was their own disobedience that gave the devil an entrance into their lives in the first place.

Promises fulfilled and rewards given come from being obedient to God's Word. Disillusionment, dissatisfaction, depression, fear, and failure all come from being disobedient: They are the offspring of disobedience.

So to achieve great faith and to receive your own personal

promised land, you must first practice obedience!

It's easy to *talk* faith! It's easy to *talk* a good fight. And there are many who have learned how to *talk* the "faith-talk." But without obedience to God and His Word, they cannot really produce anything for God!

What made Abraham the great man of faith he was? What enabled Abraham to receive the promises of God for his life, against all odds — even old age — and to receive his promised land?

We find the answer in his complete obedience to the commands of God. In Hebrews 11:8, we read, *"By faith Abraham, when he was called to go out into a place which he should after receive for an inheritance, obeyed; and he went out, not knowing whither he went."* Without even knowing where he was going, Abraham left everything to obey God!

It took complete, utter obedience and leaning on what God had said to Abraham to enter the land of promise. But Abraham obeyed, being fully persuaded that what God had said, He was also able to perform (Rom. 4:21).

Let's contrast *Abraham's obedience* with *Saul's disobedience.* Both Abraham and Saul heard the command of the Lord. Abraham chose to obey what he heard, and his life was successful because of it.

King Saul, on the other hand, heard the command of the Lord, but refused to obey. And it marked the beginning of his downfall as king of Israel. Saul refused to "hearken," as Abraham had; that is, to *hear* and *to obey*. Up to this time, Saul was very humble before God: That meant *he obeyed God*.

But by refusing to obey, Saul actually gave the devil a platform — a foothold — in his life, one from which he was never able to dislodge himself.

Finally, toward the end of Saul's career as king, he was forced to admit, ". . . *behold, I have played the fool, and have erred exceedingly*" (1 Sam. 26:21).

Do you realize the far-reaching effects of Saul's disobedience? Because of it, *Saul lost his inheritance — his promised land!*

Was it some great "catastrophe" which ultimately destroyed Saul, and over which he had no control? No! It was merely *his own* disobedience!

Also notice that this disobedience was spiritual. In other words, to begin with it wasn't gross outward sin which was readily apparent to all. Rather, it was an inward attitude of the heart that finally resulted in open rebellion to what God had commanded him to do.

Saul played the fool in not obeying God. His life ended by his own sword. Why? Did it have to be that way? Was *that* God's plan for Saul when He anointed him to be king? Emphatically no! God meant for this young man, the first king of Israel, to lead the whole nation of Israel to great heights. Yet because of disobedience, Saul lost his entire inheritance and never fulfilled the exciting things God had destined for his life.

Many Christians today are in a similar kind of disobedience, although they probably don't realize it. But it has hindered them from receiving God's best in their lives. God also has great victories He wants to lead them into! Yet for some, disobedience is the reason their prayers have not been answered, nor have the longings of their hearts been fulfilled.

It may be that God has spoken to their hearts to do something for Him, but they have flatly refused to obey. For others, it may be that they are in opposition to certain principles in God's Word, and therefore, God cannot answer their prayers *until they come into line with His Word.*

Only *you* know what God has been speaking to your heart about. All others see of you is the outward appearance, and even then, sometimes it's only what you wish to portray. No one else knows what God has told you to do.

Now at first glance, receiving God's best just by being obedient sounds so simple and easy. But upon consideration, we sometimes think that it can't possibly be *that* easy. So we go into a long drawn-out discourse with seventeen steps on how to receive from God and twenty-five more steps on how to obtain the highest kind of faith. But the highest kind of faith simply comes with one step: Complete obedience to all that God has said — "If God said it, I believe it." That's all there is to it. That's real faith — and obedience is how you get it!

I think the real problem some people may have with obedience, is that they are trying to live obedient to God on such a wide scope — on the basis of a whole lifetime — instead of just one day at a time. And the very thought of such a huge span of time lived in complete obedience, so overwhelms them that they become discouraged and feel that it's a feat too great to ever attain. They give up before they ever got started!

Now, of course, our entire life should be dedicated to God, and we should be dedicated to the fact that we are going to serve God as long as we live. However, in order to bring obedience down to a practical realm so we can relate to it, we need to think of obedience in terms of living each *moment* for God. In reality, we can't live the future today, anyway. We can only live one moment at a time — *this* very moment.

You see, if we would just concentrate on living *today* in obedience to God, then we would not have to worry about living tomorrow for God — because tomorrow hasn't come yet. And if in living *today* for God, we would just live every *moment* for Him, then we wouldn't have to be concerned about the whole day. The moment-by-moment living in obedience would take care of the whole day!

This is such an important concept to realize. We can only live in the present, in the "now" — one moment at a time. If we would just live moment-to-moment in obedience, we would find that we would always be living in the "now" of obedience!

This is exactly why some Christians never do anything for God. They are trying to accomplish things and to be obedient on such a large scope that they end up doing nothing at all for God. But by bringing it down to a daily concept, and even a moment-by-moment concept, obedience takes on an entirely different meaning. A moment-by-moment obedience is attainable to anyone!

It's so simple. Yet we have made obedience seem so difficult! *Any time we do not receive from God, we need to find out if there is any area in which we have failed to obey God.* There is never any problem with the Source; so the problem has to be with the receiver —us. Most of the time, when we fail to receive from God, there is some disobedience standing in the way, though it may be ever so subtle.

Usually, when the word "disobedience" is mentioned, everyone immediately thinks about the obvious overt sins such as lying and stealing. But the Body of Christ needs to recognize some other areas which God also sees as disobedience.

For example, not obeying God in the principles of His Word, is disobedience. When you get up grumbling in the morning, instead of praising God, *that's disobedience*. Because God said through David, *"This is the day which the Lord hath made; we WILL rejoice and be glad in it"* (Ps. 118:24).

We really disobey the Lord in ways that *we* don't think of as sin, and then we complain when we can't seem to come into all of the bountiful blessings of God.

Or, suppose someone gives you a job to do, and you're not as qualified as you feel you should be. Complaining that you are not qualified is *disobedience*. Why? Because in my Bible it says, "*I can do all things through Christ which strengtheneth me*" (Phil. 4:13). Notice that it says ALL things — not just spiritual things, but *all* things.

Another area that Christians may fail to recognize as disobedience, is the area of doubt. In the Old Testament, when the people doubted and refused to believe God to take them into Canaan, God called that an "evil report." They couldn't enter their promised land with an evil report, and neither can you!

The promises of God have already been given to you. They contain all the good things that are yours by inheritance. But you will have to believe them, and completely obey God, in order to receive them. And you will have to go back to where you missed it, and get back in line with God and His Word before you will qualify as "willing and obedient" (Isa. 1:19).

If you really believe what God said, then you will obey Him. And you will receive from Him whatever you need!

Chapter 4
Disobedience and
How To Deal With It

This brings us to the final point in this study of obedience. We cannot fully deal with obedience without dealing with disobedience. An individual who is obedient in some areas, for example, may find himself disobedient in other areas. How is this corrected? What do you do? How do you keep yourself from getting depressed because you're in disobedience? How do you keep the devil from using it against you and causing you even more heartache than you already have?

The Lord, through Jeremiah the prophet said, "... *Return, thou backsliding Israel, saith the Lord ... for I am merciful ... Only acknowledge thine iniquity, that thou hast transgressed against the Lord thy God . . . and ye have not obeyed my voice . . . Turn, O backsliding children, saith the Lord . . ."* (Jer. 3:12-14).

Although this was written originally to the nation of Israel, there is a modern-day application for us. The Body of Christ needs to recognize our shortcomings, and admit — first to ourselves — those areas where we have failed to obey God. This means we should have a keener awareness and conviction *of what God calls sin*. Then we will have to confess wholeheartedly any disobedience to His will. That's simple; it doesn't have to be done on a platform in front of everyone. It has to be done between you and God. And with that confession should come a more profound commitment to live for God.

Be aware, however, that if you confess these things to God with a lax attitude, you will get into more trouble than you were in to begin with. Beware of those kinds of confessions that simply come from your head and not your heart. If you don't really want to confess your mistakes in the first place, you will just be following a form.

This is the same as making a faith confession out of the head rather than the heart. A head confession, faithwise, is about as spiritually fruitful as saying, "Twinkle, twinkle little star; how I wonder what you are." It's just as true with confessing your disobedience from the head only; then it's only coming from the natural realm. It won't do you any good — it won't change you any if it doesn't come from the heart.

If you'll read God's Word from cover to cover, you'll find that God never tolerated disobedience. He has trouble with disobedient people. You see, disobedience to God will carry a penalty. It carried a penalty in the Old Testament as well as in the New. Sooner or later, the disobedient were called to a reckoning. And in every case they had to start over in obedience to God and His laws before they could go on with Him.

So every time you find *obedience*, you will find *repentance*. Obedience and repentance go hand-in-hand. And if the Body of Christ would just learn to correct and judge themselves, God would not have to do it. But if we don't obey, then God is duty bound by His Word to judge us. Actually, *we bring it on ourselves* by our own disobedience.

So we can see that the way to avoid the judgment of God, is to judge ourselves in our disobedience to Him, and repent. But how can we keep from continually finding ourselves in these areas of disobedience? What's our safeguard?

If there's anything causing problems in the Body of Christ today and keeping the Church from complete obedience, it is a lack of personal devotion time. Yet this is the believer's safeguard against continually falling into the same areas of disobedience. Sadly, preachers as well as laypeople are guilty of neglecting personal devotion time.

Some preachers make the excuse that they are studying the Word all the time. Yes, they're studying the Word continually for their sermons. But that can never take the place of personal devotion time.

Our day needs to begin with the Lord. That is where we will get our power and victory for the day. And it is where God's love and strength will be fed into our very lives, so that we will be able to overcome anything that would try to come against us during the day!

In your devotion time — *dialogue* with God. Complete communication is not just a monologue. Get quiet after you talk to God, so that you can hear what *He* wants to say to you. So many Christians miss blessings that God had planned for them that day, because they don't stop long enough to listen to Him!

Real prayer (not monologue, but dialogue with God), ushers the believer into the very Presence of God. It makes him secure in his relationship with God and keeps him in God's Presence the whole day long.

Now some people think that they must get a tingly feeling all over to let them know they are in God's Presence. This is where a lot of Christians get whipped. They think, *Well, I must not have gotten into God's Presence this morning because I didn't feel a thing.* That has nothing to do with it! If you're a child of God, walking in fellowship with Him, you're in His Presence whether you feel anything or not. But a deep communion with God in your devotions will allow you to know *His* Presence, and to actually live in His Presence throughout your day.

There is a second thing that is involved in complete obedience to God: That is Bible reading. Now you might say, "Oh, I've heard all that before." But let's look at it from a little different angle.

First, to receive completely from what you read in the Word of God, you are going to have to be in complete surrender each day to obey God. Each day as you begin to study His Word, say, "Lord, here I am today. Once again, it is my desire to be in complete obedience to *Your will* for me today." Then begin to praise and worship God. Why? Because a study of the Word of God will show that the greatest attitude with which to approach God and to receive Him, is the attitude of praise and worship. The Word says that praise and worship ascend unto the Heavenly Father as a sweet-smelling savor. It opens God's heart of compassion, and He just opens His arms wider and pours out more blessings.

There are many times when God's people walk into the house of God, sing all the familiar choruses, raise their hands, and praise God. Yet, it cannot ascend to God as a sweet-smelling savor because there is no obedience to go along with it! God's people cannot worship in spirit and in truth with disobedience in their hearts! Many times the reason we're not receiving from God is because disobedience nullifies all of our praise. But when we practice obedience and *we* worship God, we cannot help but please the Heavenly Father.

Once you have surrendered your will to God, and have come to Him in an attitude of praise and worship, then you are ready to receive completely from His Word.

It is in this attitude that you will discover what King David meant when he said that God's Words were ". . . *sweeter also than honey and the honeycomb.*" He also said, *"More to be desired are they than gold, yea, than much fine gold . . ."* (Ps. 19:10). When you understand the sweetness of God's Words, obedience will become more natural to you and more refreshing to your spirit than food is to your body. That's when obedience becomes so delightful that you wouldn't think of doing anything else!

We need to understand just why personal Bible study is so vital to the believer. Christians have to be in God's Word to get their minds renewed and to come in line with it. The natural man, the man on the outside, does not want to come in line with God's Word, nor to any discipline. The natural man likes to do just as he pleases, without having to answer to anyone.

The natural man, with his natural mind, has not yet been renewed, transformed, or reborn. That's why Paul said that the man on the inside has to continually keep the man on the outside "under," or, *under control*. That means that the spiritual man on the inside has to keep *the mind* under subjection, or it will run wild because *it* is still in contact

with this world where the devil is
god of this world (2 Cor. 4:4).

The whole creation groans,
according to Romans chapter 8,
for the day when all of creation
will be set free and come under
the Lordship and Headship of
God once again. Then, not only
born-again believers — but all
creation — will come back under
the complete supremacy of God,
the way it was in the beginning.

You see, the Word of God
makes people come in line with
discipline. *And it is only through
the Word that man can bring his
mind into subjection to the Lordship of Jesus Christ.* There can
be no obedience without it!

Obedience, then, is fellow-
shipping with God in His perfect
will — the Word of God. Without
obedience there can be no spiritual power to enter into the
knowledge of God. So many
people want to tap into the deep,

hidden riches of God's Word. Yet very few are willing to pay the price. Obedience is part of that price. God can trust the obedient one and can reveal to him the secret things because God knows that person will obey Him when He tells him to do something. Many people pray and fast for God to show them rich spiritual truths; yet if they would just start obeying Him in the simple things, He would trust them with the secret things.

Without obedience, there is no confidence that God will do for you what you're asking Him to do (John 15:7; 1 John 3:20-22; John 8:31,32). According to His Word, He can't until you come in line with Him. Without obedience, there is no boldness on your part. Without obedience there is no liberty.

A lot of people call obedience "bondage." No, obedience sets you free. Obedience liberates. Obedience give you an arena in which to operate where there are no hindrances; there is no wondering what will happen to you, because the power of God surrounds you. God takes up the petition of the obedient one!

Bondage comes when there's disobedience. That's when the heaviness, fear, and guilt come. They are in the arena of disobedience. But when there is complete obedience, there is no fear. There is no guilt. There is liberty, joy, and happiness.

If the Body of Christ would grasp the importance of a lifestyle committed to obedience, it would absolutely transform lives!

Whatever you need from God will be simply received by believing and obeying Him. Get in line with God's Word and everything will work for you!

If we are ever going to be the Church that God has called us to be in this generation, we must come to grips with complete obedience to His will.

We can talk all we want about how much we love God, and how much we're serving Him, but unless we are submitted to His laws and His Word in complete obedience, we don't really love Him nearly as much as we think we do. The true test of love for God is how much we obey what His Word says (John 14:15,21)!

I believe the unspeakable riches of God will come to the Body of Christ and will become a part of our lives, as we learn — and put into practice — the simple truth of obedience.

Build your life on obedience to God!

A Sinner's Prayer To Receive Jesus as Savior

Dear Heavenly Father,

I come to You in the Name of Jesus.

Your Word says, *". . . him that cometh to me I will in no wise cast out"* (John 6:37),

So I know You won't cast me out, but You take me in,

And I thank You for it.

You said in Your Word, *"Whosoever shall call upon the name of the Lord shall be saved"* (Rom. 10:13).

I am calling on Your name,

So I know You have saved me now.

You also said, *". . . if thou shalt confess with thy mouth the Lord Jesus, and shalt believe in thine heart that God hath raised him from the dead, thou shalt be saved. For with the heart man believeth unto righteousness; and with the mouth confession is made unto salvation"* (Rom. 10:9,10).

I believe in my heart that Jesus Christ is the Son of God.

I believe that He was raised from the dead for my justification.

And I confess Him now as my Lord,

Because Your Word says, "*. . .with the heart man believeth unto righteousness . . .*" and I do believe with my heart,

I have now become the righteousness of God in Christ (2 Cor. 5:21),

And I am saved!

Thank You, Lord!

Signed _____

Date _____

About the Author

Kenneth Hagin Jr., Executive Vice-President of Kenneth Hagin Ministries and Pastor of RHEMA Bible Church, teaches from a rich and diversified background of more than 35 years in the ministry.

Rev. Hagin Jr. attended Southwestern Assemblies of God College and graduated from Oral Roberts University with a degree in religious education. He also holds an honorary Doctor of Divinity degree from Faith Theological Seminary in Tampa, Florida.

After serving as an associate pastor, Rev. Hagin Jr. traveled as an evangelist throughout the United States and abroad and was responsible for organizing RHEMA Bible Training Center, a school which equips men and women for the ministry.

In addition to his administrative and teaching responsibilities at RHEMA, Rev. Hagin Jr. is pastor of RHEMA Bible Church, a large, thriving congregation on the RHEMA campus. He is also International Director of RHEMA Ministerial Association International, has a weekly radio program, "RHEMA Radio Church," which is heard on stations throughout the United States, and a television program, "RHEMA Praise."